D1706959

ROW! GARDENING
PLANTING

by Rebecca Pettiford

rogo

Ideas for Parents and Teachers

Pogo Books let children practice reading informational text while introducing them to nonfiction features such as headings, labels, sidebars, maps, and diagrams, as well as a table of contents, glossary, and index.

Carefully leveled text with a strong photo match offers early fluent readers the support they need to succeed.

Before Reading

- "Walk" through the book and point out the various nonfiction features. Ask the student what purpose each feature serves.
- Look at the glossary together. Read and discuss the words.

Read the Book

- Have the child read the book independently.
- Invite him or her to list questions that arise from reading.

After Reading

- Discuss the child's questions. Talk about how he or she might find answers to those questions.
- Prompt the child to think more. Ask: Have you ever planted a seed? Did it grow? If so, what did it become?

Pogo Books are published by Jump!
5357 Penn Avenue South
Minneapolis, MN 55419
www.jumplibrary.com

Library of Congress Cataloging-in-Publication Data

Pettiford, Rebecca, author.
 Planting / by Rebecca Pettiford.
    pages cm. – (Way to grow! Gardening)
 Includes index.
 ISBN 978-1-62031-228-5 (hardcover: alk. paper) –
 ISBN 978-1-62496-315-5 (ebook)
 1. Gardening–Juvenile literature. I. Title. II. Series:
 Pettiford, Rebecca. Way to grow! Gardening.
 SB457.P48 2015
 635–dc23

                                      2015000279

Series Editor: Jenny Fretland VanVoorst
Series Designer: Anna Peterson
Photo Researcher: Anna Peterson

Photo Credits: All photos by Shutterstock except:
Corbis, 18–19; Thinkstock, cover, 12–13, 16–17.

Printed in the United States of America at
Corporate Graphics in North Mankato, Minnesota.

TABLE OF CONTENTS

CHAPTER 1

LET'S PLANT A GARDEN!

It's spring. Let's plant a garden!

It's fun and easy to grow colorful flowers, scented **herbs**, and healthy food.

Where will you plant your garden? Most plants need a lot of sunlight. Find a space in your yard that faces south. It gets the most sun.

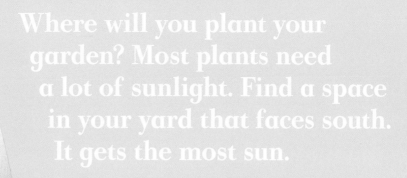

DID YOU KNOW?

Don't have room for a garden? If your town has a community garden, ask a parent or guardian if you can get space there.

Before you can plant outside, you need to **till** the soil. This gets it ready for planting. Don't forget to dig up weeds. They can make your plants weak.

garden fork

CHAPTER 2

SOWING SEEDS

You start a garden by **sowing** seeds.

When do you start it? It depends on where you live.

You can start some seeds in the garden.
You can start other seeds inside.

To learn the best planting time for your
area, visit a library or garden center.
You can also look it up on the Internet.

seedling

Some seeds need a thin layer of soil. Others need to be planted deeper. Your seed packet will tell you how deep to plant your seeds. It will tell you how much water and light they need.

Soon the seeds will **germinate**. Young plants are called **seedlings**.

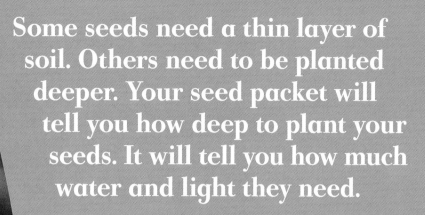

DID YOU KNOW?

A greenhouse is a special building for growing plants. It usually has walls of glass or plastic to absorb sunlight. A greenhouse can make a growing season longer. It also lets you keep plants that do not grow easily where you live.

CHAPTER 3

CARING FOR PLANTS

Plants need healthy soil to grow. To add more **nutrients** to the soil, you can make your own **compost**. It is made of dead plants like leaves and grass.

compost

Add **mulch** to help control weeds and retain moisture.

mulch

Fertilizer can help plants grow faster. Compost is an **organic** fertilizer. It adds nutrients to the soil.

Some gardeners use **mineral** fertilizers. A slow-release fertilizer releases its nutrients as the plant grows. This gives the plant what it needs during its growth cycle.

mineral fertilizer

Just like you, plants need water. Water moves nutrients through the plant. Some plants need more water than others.

DID YOU KNOW?

Planting certain flowers, herbs, or vegetables near others can be good for both plants. For example, gardeners often plant strawberries and bush beans together. Bush beans add nutrients to the soil that strawberries need. And strawberry plants repel pests that damage bush beans.

You play a big part in your garden's success. Find a sunny spot for it. Plant when the time is right. Make sure the soil is healthy. Water your garden. Before you know it, it will be time to **harvest** your plants!

ACTIVITIES & TOOLS

HOW DOES SOIL AFFECT PLANT GROWTH?

Soil contains the nutrients plants need to grow. But does all soil have the same nutrients in the same amounts? Are some soils better for growing than others? Let's find out.

What You Need:
- three plastic cups
- tray
- three or more seeds
- soil from three different places

❶ Poke several small holes on the bottom of each cup. Put the cups in the tray.

❷ Fill the cups with soil, each with soil from a different place. Label the cups by soil type (for example, yard, park, school).

❸ Water the soil lightly. Plant the same type and number of seeds in each cup.

❹ Put the tray near a sunny window. Wait three to 14 days.

❺ Add water to the tray so the plants can drink.

❻ What happened? Did your seeds prefer one soil to another? Why do you think so?

GLOSSARY

compost: A rotted mix of plants like leaves and grass that makes garden soil healthy.

fertilizer: Material that is added to the soil to help plants grow.

germinate: To begin to grow.

harvest: To gather crops such as fruits and vegetables.

herbs: Plants that add flavor to food or are used to make perfume and medicine.

mineral: Material that occurs naturally in the ground but is not living.

mulch: Dead leaves or wood chips that you spread around a plant to help the soil and control weeds.

nutrients: Food or other elements that help plants grow and stay healthy.

organic: Made from materials that were once living.

seedlings: Young plants grown from seed.

sowing: Planting seeds.

till: To get the soil ready for planting.

INDEX

TO LEARN MORE

Learning more is as easy as 1, 2, 3.

1) **Go to www.factsurfer.com**

2) **Enter "planting" into the search box.**

3) **Click the "Surf" to see a list of websites.**

With factsurfer, finding more information is just a click away.